MW01129627

# WHERE ELSE DO BABIES COME FROM?

A family guide to assisted reproduction

WRITTEN BY
HOPE A. C. BENTLEY

ILLUSTRATED BY
KATE RENNER

To Nancy and Debby, who are mothers to me
and
Erin and Elly, who are mothers with me.
-HB

To Dr. Peter Casson, who solved the mystery.
-KR

Published by
Golden Light Factory
East Burke, Vermont
www.goldenlightfactory.com

ISBN 978-1-7327645-1-4

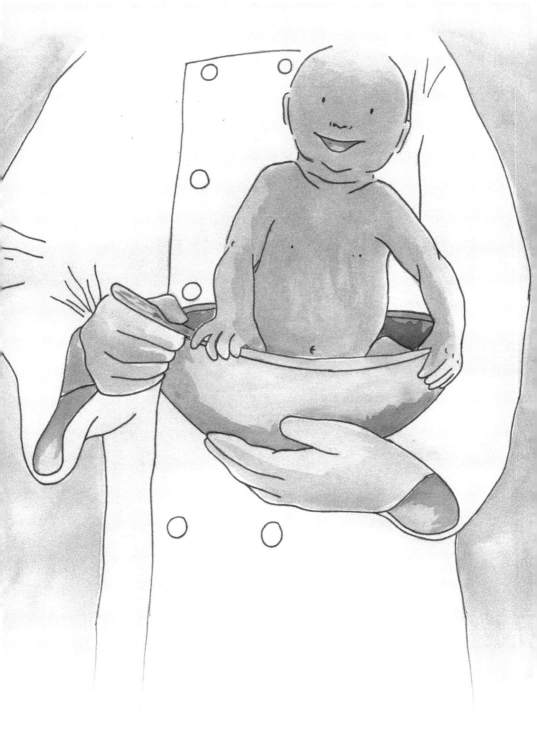

To make a baby,
you need four ingredients:

a healthy egg from a woman,

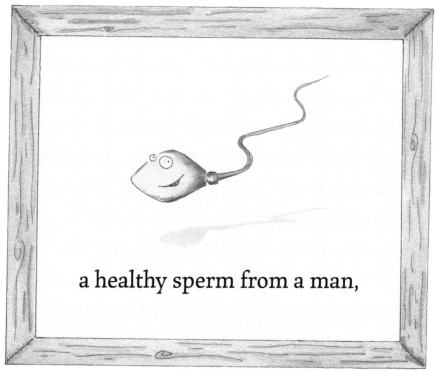

a healthy sperm from a man,

a woman's healthy uterus,

and...

MYSTERY.*

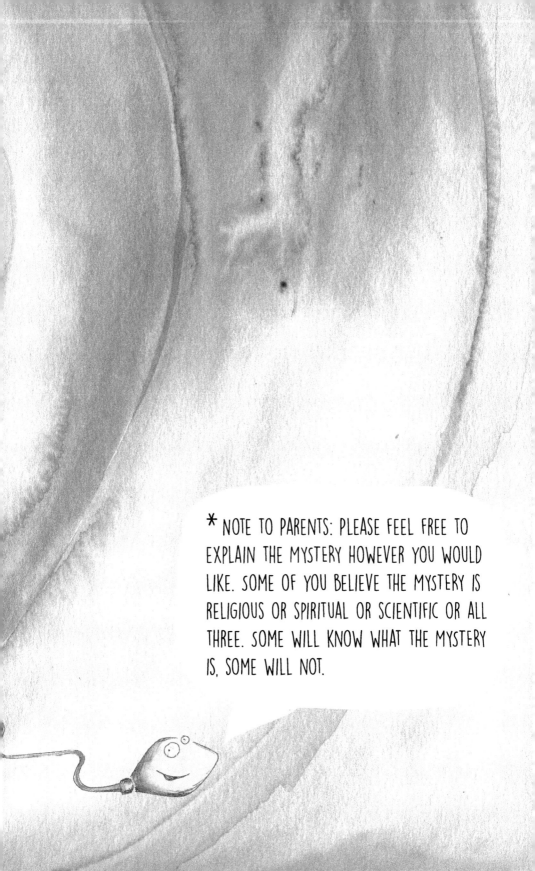

\* NOTE TO PARENTS: PLEASE FEEL FREE TO EXPLAIN THE MYSTERY HOWEVER YOU WOULD LIKE. SOME OF YOU BELIEVE THE MYSTERY IS RELIGIOUS OR SPIRITUAL OR SCIENTIFIC OR ALL THREE. SOME WILL KNOW WHAT THE MYSTERY IS, SOME WILL NOT.

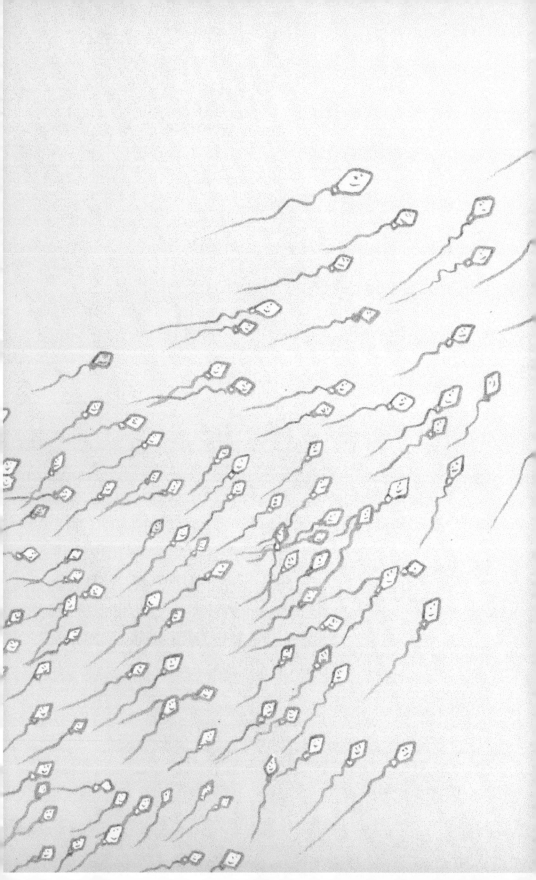

OVER HERE,
GUYS!

For thousands of years, people have
been making babies like this: A man
and a woman put their private parts
together. Sperm comes out of the
man's penis and travels up the
woman's vagina to the egg.

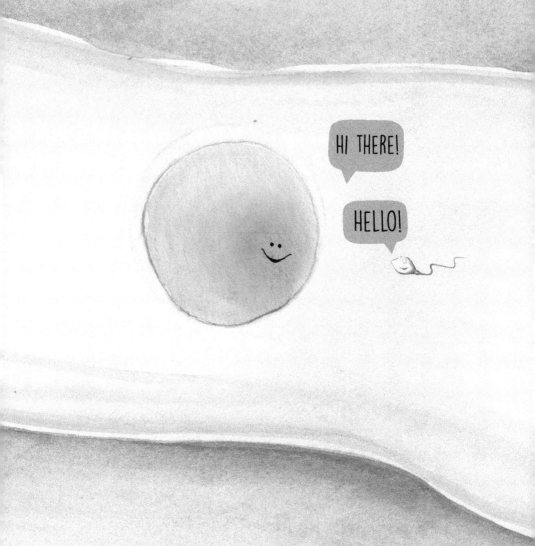

The healthiest sperm introduces itself, and together they become a zygote. The zygote drifts down to the uterus, where the woman's body helps it grow into a baby.

But sometimes something doesn't work.

Or a family is missing some of the ingredients.

THIS FAMILY HAS EGGS, SPERM, AND A UTERUS, BUT THEY CAN'T FIND THE MYSTERY ANYWHERE.

THIS FAMILY HAS SPERM, BUT
THEY NEED AN EGG AND A
UTERUS.

Sometimes the problem is easy to solve.

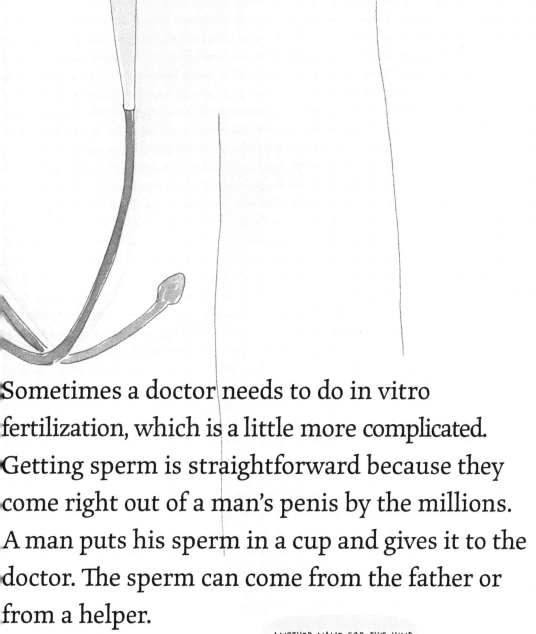

Sometimes a doctor needs to do in vitro fertilization, which is a little more complicated. Getting sperm is straightforward because they come right out of a man's penis by the millions. A man puts his sperm in a cup and gives it to the doctor. The sperm can come from the father or from a helper.

ANOTHER NAME FOR THIS KIND OF HELPER IS SPERM DONOR.

If a family needs a healthy egg, it can come from the mother or from a helper.

ANOTHER NAME FOR THIS KIND OF HELPER IS EGG DONOR.

Getting eggs is tricky because eggs need to be taken out of a woman's body by a doctor at exactly the right time.

Helpers might be people the family knows well, or they might be somebody they have never met.

Usually parents will read about helpers and choose the one who sounds right for them.

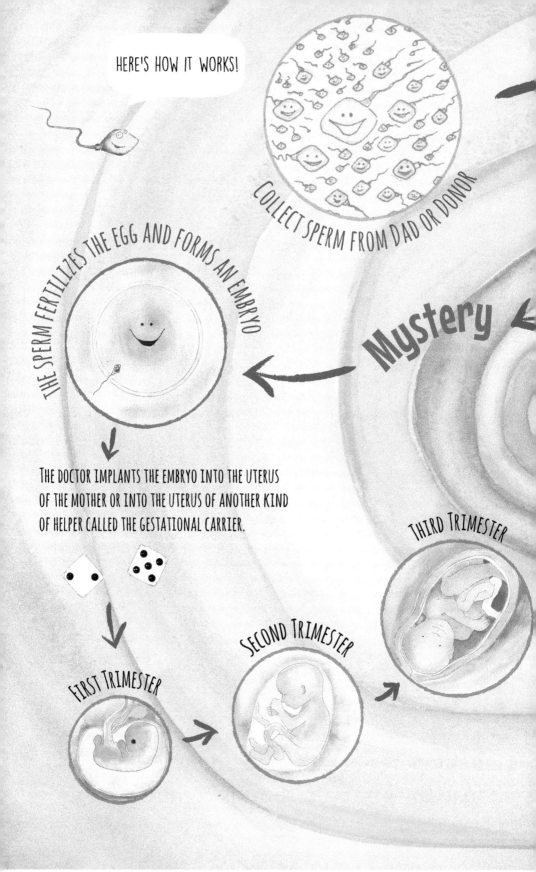

COLLECT EGGS FROM MOM OR DONOR

PUT THE EGG AND THE SPERM TOGETHER

HELLO, BABY!

You might need just two people to make a
baby...

or many!  However a baby is made....

the most important ingredient is

# Further resources:

### RESOLVE: The National Infertility Association
*www.resolve.org*
RESOLVE covers the gamut. Volunteering opportunities, legislation to watch out for, support groups, information, counseling; you name it, they've got it.

### Reproductive Facts by the American Society for Reproductive Medicine
*www.reproductivefacts.org*
All the science, all the facts about the nitty gritty of reproduction and assisted reproduction.

### The Academy of Adoption and Assisted Reproduction Attorneys
*www.adoptionart.org*
AAAA is an organization of nearly 500 highly vetted attorneys dedicated to the competent and ethical practice of adoption and assisted reproduction law.

CPSIA information can be obtained
at www.ICGtesting.com
Printed in the USA
BVHW022036050219
539580BV00002B/2/P

9 781732 764514